Real Life Stories

THE WAGON TRAIN

Jill Bryant

— Weigl Publishers Inc. —

About *The Wagon Train*
This book is based on the real life accounts of the people who settled the American West. History is brought to life through quotes from personal journals, letters to family back home, and historical records of those who traveled West to build a better life.

Published by Weigl Publishers Inc.
123 South Broad Street, Box 227
Mankato, MN 56002
USA

Web site: www.weigl.com

Library of Congress Cataloging-in-Publication Data

Bryant, Jill.
    The wagon train / by Jill Bryant.
        p. cm. -- (Real life stories series)
    Summary: Briefly explores what it was like to travel across the country by wagon train, including first-hand accounts about such things as cooking on the trail and dangers to be faced.
    Includes bibliographical references and index.
    ISBN 1-59036-082-6 (library bound : alk. paper)
    1. Frontier and pioneer life--West (U.S.)--Juvenile literature.   2. Overland journeys to the Pacific--Juvenile literature. 3. Pioneers--West (U.S.)--History--19th century--Juvenile literature.
    4. West (U.S.)--History--19th century--Juvenile literature.   5. West (U.S.)--Social life and customs--19th century--Juvenile literature.   [1. Frontier and pioneer life--West (U.S.) 2. Over- land journeys to the Pacific. 3. Pioneers--West (U.S.) 4. West (U.S.)--History. 5. West (U.S.)--Social life and customs.]   I. Title. II. Series.
    F596.B88 2003
    978'.02--dc21
                                        2002012727

Printed in the United States of America
1 2 3 4 5 6 7 8 9 0   06 05 04 03 02

Project Coordinator	**Copy Editor**	**Layout**
Michael Lowry	Frances Purslow	Terry Paulhus
Substantive Editor	**Design**	**Photo Research**
Christa Bedry	Virginia Boulay & Bryan Pezzi	Dylan Kirk & Daorcey Le Bray

Contents

Safety in Numbers

People used covered wagons to travel across America years ago. The wagons traveled in groups called wagon trains. Wagon trains were made up of family members and friends. It was safer to travel in groups for the travelers in the wagon trains.

Most **settlers** left the east in the springtime. They wanted to arrive in the West before the first snowfall. The journey lasted 4 to 6 months. Each group chose one guide and one captain who would lead the wagon train to the end of the journey.

As many as 100 wagons traveled in one wagon train. The leader of a wagon train was called the wagon boss.

The Covered Wagon

Having enough water could mean the difference between life and death. A water barrel often sat on a shelf on the side of the wagon.

Travel Supplies

Settlers had to pack enough food for the long journey. They also had to take dishes, cooking pots, buckets, rope, furniture, and clothing. Bedding, such as blankets, quilts, and pillows, were taken on the trail. A **spinning wheel** and a camp stove were important. Spare parts for the wagon, a rifle, an ax, and basic farm tools were also loaded into the wagons. Some travelers took farm animals along.

Settlers read wagon-travel guidebooks to help them choose which supplies to pack. What would you take on a 6-month trip to a new home?

Real Life Stories

"In [packing] supplies for this journey, the emigrant should provide himself with, at least, 200 pounds of flour, 150 pounds of bacon, 10 pounds of coffee, 20 pounds of sugar, and 10 pounds of salt."

Lansford Hastings

Wake-Up Call

Settlers awoke before sunrise. They ate a quick breakfast. Then, they prepared to leave. A bugle sounded. The guide and the captain made sure that the wagons were ready. The wagon train was moving by 7:00 AM. The wagons were so full that most people walked beside them.

Settlers cooked their food over a campfire using iron pots and frying pans.

Real Life Stories

"In the morning, as soon as the day breaks, the first that we hear is the words, 'Arise! Arise!'—then the mules set up such a noise … which puts the whole camp in motion. We encamp in a large ring, baggage and men, tents and wagons on the outside, and all the animals except the cows, which are fastened to pickets, within the circle."

Narcissa Whitman

Daily Life

Everyone enjoyed a cold lunch at noon. The women had made the lunches in the morning. The adults talked, and the children played. The oxen and other animals rested.

The wagons stopped again in the late afternoon. They formed a large ring. The women cooked and set up the bedding inside the ring. They also **mended** and washed the clothes. The men repaired the wagons and took care of the animals.

Guards kept watch at night. They protected the settlers and the supplies.

Real Life Stories

"We did not know the dangers we were going through. The idea of my father was to get on the coast: no other place suited him, and he went right ahead until he got there."

Martha Ann Morrison

The Covered Wagon

Covered wagons were often called prairie **schooners**. This was because they looked like sailboats. The round, canvas roofs looked like sails blowing in the wind. The wagons could travel 12 to 20 miles on a good day. The wagons covered less than 5 miles on days when the weather was poor or the ground was rough.

Wooden ribs curved over the wagon box. The canvas roof was then stretched over them.

Wagon boxes were small and light. Wagon boxes could carry 2,500 pounds. They were about 10 feet long. The box sides were about 2 feet high.

The front wheels were smaller than the back wheels. This helped the wagon make sharp turns on mountain trails.

Many wagons had a toolbox built onto the side. Tools were handy when wagons broke down on the trail.

White canvas was stretched over the wagon to protect the supplies from the sun and the rain. The cover was drawn tight at each end to keep out the dust.

Cooking on the Trail

The women cooked all the meals outdoors. Breakfast included coffee or tea, bacon, dry bread or pancakes, and fried meat or beans. Lunch was usually coffee or tea served with cold beans and bacon. Dried fruit was sometimes added to a meal. This helped prevent **scurvy**. The men hunted and fished for food. This was a welcome change from the dried or salted meat that was eaten daily.

The women could often only cook at night. This meant that breakfast and lunch were both served cold.

Real Life Stories

"It is very trying on the patience to cook and bake on a little green wood fire with the smoke blowing in your eyes so as to blind you, and shivering with cold so as to make the teeth chatter."

Esther Hannah

A Hard Road to Travel

Settlers traveled through terrible weather, biting mosquitoes, and thieving rats. Many settlers did not reach the western **frontier**. They died of diseases such as **cholera** and **smallpox**. Other travelers turned back home. They were discouraged by the challenges on the trail. Settlers who finished the journey felt a great sense of pride.

Steep mountain passes were one of the many dangers faced by settlers on the wagon trails.

Real Life Stories

"This morning was dry, dusty, and sandy. This afternoon it rained, hailed, and the wind was very high. Have been traveling all the afternoon in mud and water up to our hubs. Broke chains and stuck in the mud several times."

Amelia Stewart Knight

Main Routes West

There were many trails that led to the West. The Oregon Trail was the most well-known of the westward trails. The California Trail broke off from the Oregon Trail and carried gold seekers to San Francisco. The Santa Fe Trail was used mainly for trade. The Mormon Trail was named for the thousands of **Mormons** who moved to new homes. The Butterfield Trail brought stagecoaches West. The stagecoaches carried mail and passengers.

Oxen were best suited to pull the wagons. Oxen could eat the prairie grasses and were very strong. Four to six oxen pulled one covered wagon.

Trails to the West

Oregon City

San Francisco

Salt Lake City

Fort Laramie

Council Bluffs

Nauvoo

Los Angeles

Santa Fe

Independence

Mississippi River

N W E S

Key

Oregon Trail

California Trail

Butterfield Trail

Mormon Trail

Santa Fe Trail

City ●

Scale in Miles

0   250   500

Learning More about the Wagon Train

To learn more about the wagon train, you can borrow books from the library or surf the Internet.

Books

Johmann, Carol A. and Elizabeth J. Rieth. *Going West! Journey on a Wagon Train to Settle a Frontier Town*. Charlotte: Williamson Publishing Company, 2000.

Kramer, Sydelle A. and Deborah Kogan Ray. *Wagon Train*. New York: Putnam Publishing Group, 2002.

Web Sites

Oregon National Historic Trail
www.nps.gov/oreg/
This Web site contains information for park visitors interested in exploring the Oregon Trail.

Encarta
www.encarta.com
Enter the search words "wagon train" into an online encyclopedia, such as Encarta.

Different Viewpoints

Imagine you are the guide of a wagon train. At a river crossing, someone spots a sign on a tree that says "Shortcut This Way." The arrow points away from the river. Many of the people in your group want to take the shortcut. Shortcuts can be very dangerous. They can take longer than the main route. What do you do? List reasons for taking the shortcut and not taking the shortcut.

What Have You Learned?

Based on what you have just read, try to answer the following questions.

1 When did most wagon trains begin their journey?

a) the fall
b) mid-summer
c) the spring
d) January 1

2 True or false? Settlers always enjoyed a hot lunch on the trail.

3 Dried fruit was eaten to prevent which of the following illnesses?

a) scurvy
b) cholera
c) tooth decay
d) smallpox

4 At what time did the wagon train usually begin moving in the morning?

a) 5:00
b) 11:00
c) 7:00
d) 8:00

5 True or false? Many emigrants died of cholera and smallpox.

6 True or false? Covered wagons traveled as far as 20 miles on a good day.

Answers

1. c
2. False. Settlers ate a cold lunch, which was prepared in the morning.
3. a
4. c
5. True
6. True

Words to Know

cholera: disease of the stomach and intestines that causes vomiting, cramps, and diarrhea

frontier: land that has not yet been developed

mended: repaired, often by sewing

Mormons: members of the Mormon church

schooners: sailing ships with two or more masts

scurvy: a disease caused by the lack of vitamin C

settlers: people who set up their homes in a new region

smallpox: a disease that causes fevers and blisters

spinning wheel: a machine that spins flax, wool, or cotton into yarn or thread

Index